G000243301

I wanted to wra
pinning both en..
with palm rib slivers.

mpT
MODERN POETRY
IN TRANSLATION
The best of world poetry

No. 3 2022
© *Modern Poetry in Translation* 2022 and contributors

ISSN (print) 0969-3572
ISSN (online) 2052-3017
ISBN (print) 978-1-910485-34-7

Editor: Khairani Barokka
Managing Editor: Sarah Hesketh
Digital Content Editor: Ed Cottrell
Finance Manager: Deborah de Kock
Creative Apprentice: Dom Green
Design by Brett Evans Biedscheid
Cover art by Pratya Aprilana
Typesetting by Libanus Press Ltd

Printed and bound in Great Britain by Charlesworth Press, Wakefield
For submissions and subscriptions please visit www.modernpoetryintranslation.com

Modern Poetry in Translation Limited. A Company Limited by Guarantee Registered
in England and Wales, Number 5881603 UK Registered Charity Number 1118223

Cover description: On the front, the *MPT* logo and 'WRAP IT IN BANANA
LEAVES: THE FOOD FOCUS', with an illustration of tumpeng, the Indonesian
rice dish cooked for celebrations – a yellow rice cone with the point wrapped in
banana leaves, surrounded by various foods including eggs and tofu at its base,
also covered in banana leaves. The tumpeng is set on a table. The back cover shows
the names of all contributors, with an extension of that table, on which is set a
spoon and sambal in a bowl. The cover is in shades of orange, brown and yellow.
Illustrator: Pratya Aprilana.

Supported using public funding by
ARTS COUNCIL
ENGLAND
LOTTERY FUNDED

MODERN POETRY IN TRANSLATION

Wrap It in Banana Leaves
The Food Focus

CONTENTS

Focus

Reviews

EDITORIAL

Food is culture, and poetry chronicles our engagement with what nourishes or destroys. In the Food Focus that follows are diverse paradigms for taste, cooking, communality, memory, and preservation of cultural heritage. Whilst structures of capital are working to detach us from all the many people and steps it takes to create a meal, poetry can centre our relationships to them.

Against enforced mass homogeneity of foodways through industrial, destructive agricultural policies, in poetry we find pluralities of cosmologies, phenomenologies, and sensorial modes and paradigms for the edible. It is an immense honour to take on the mantle of *MPT* Editor, following the dedicated and passionate work of Clare Pollard, and editors before her; I could not have asked for a more enjoyable way to begin the position of my dreams than with this issue, in which you'll find all of the above.

It is our utmost pleasure to present to you poems that give us an undeniable sense of place, bubbling emotions, a zest for the whimsical . . . Or a poetic banquet so mouthwatering – as you'll read in Salma Harland's remarkable translation of Kushajim, and accompanying essay – that it caused an Abbasid caliph to command it be cooked for him.

Here are poets who've passed on and left their poetic feasts for us; in this issue, besides Kushajim, we find Birendra Chattopadhyay, Ingeborg Bachmann, and Federico García Lorca. Alongside them are a cornucopia of living poets, each with a distinct take, chosen here for providing necessary perspectives and linguistic choices that stray from clichés.

Jhio Jan Navarro's Hiligaynon verse, in Eric Abalajon's translation, and Thila Varghese's translation of S. Vijayalakshmi's Tamil poems both provide indispensable, beautifully-rendered poems of witness to how colonial, capitalist policies change communities and individual farmers. While Şafak Sarıçiçek

mpT
**MODERN POETRY
IN TRANSLATION**
The best of world poetry

'ANYONE WHO WANTS TO CHANGE THE WORLD AND SEE IT CHANGED SHOULD JOIN MPT'

– John Berger

Founded by Ted Hughes and Daniel Weissbort in 1965, *MPT* publishes the best world poetry in the best English translations, alongside reviews and essays that explore what it means to be a citizen of the world.

£23 a year – UK Subscription
£33 – International Subscription
3 print issues a year and full access to thousands of poems

To read the best in world poetry
and to subscribe:

 @MPTmagazine

 facebook.com/MPT.Magazine/

www.modernpoetryintranslation.com

Supported using public funding by
**ARTS COUNCIL
ENGLAND**

and Teemu Helle, translated by Csilla Toldy and Niina Pollari respectively, frame food in delightfully speculative, un-realist fashion.

We are introducing a new Language Justice Column in each issue, to contextualise our words in ethics. And we could not be happier to kickstart it with N.A. Mansour's 'Faqoos' essay, with its narrative showing us how we can hold foods as sociopolitical, with emotional heft, and our words with considered intention.

Whether reading a fruit poem from the sole remaining speaker of the Min 'a Leá dialect of Donegal – Cathal Ó Searcaigh translated by Gabriel Rosenstock – or a translation of Lena Yau, who specialises in food poetry, by transnational collective Colaboratorio Ávila, we are reminded of the myriad ways in which we can preserve, connect through, and shape language.

Expecting a diversity of foodways to show up in the large spread of submissions, I was nonetheless consistently surprised by the sheer range of approaches to this Focus. The poems here will take you in directions tragicomic, surreal, earthy, gritty, tender, true – their ingredients are simply delicious.

There are fantastic poems outside the Food Focus as well, beginning with Hirondina Joshua's exhilarating invitation, translated by Grant Schutzman, and Humberto Ak'abal's gorgeous poems on the natural world, translated by Michael Bazzett.

Opposite: In black and white, various photographs of various former MPT contributors in three rows of six. Below is the MPT logo and motto, 'The best of world poetry', alongside a quote from John Berger, saying 'ANYONE WHO WANTS TO SEE THE WORLD AND SEE IT CHANGED SHOULD JOIN MPT'. Below that is the ACE logo, as well as a line describing MPT, our social media information, website, and subscription info (£23 a year – UK Subscription, £33 – International Subscription).

Jhumpa Lahiri's remarkable project in Italian, *Nerina's Notebook* is excerpted, in the poet's translation, alongside an interview with her yielding many gems. We wrap up the issue (in banana leaves, of course) with excellent reviews by Esther Kondo Heller and Mayada Ibrahim.

Food, of course, is indelibly tied to sustenance, to fuel, to keeping things going. An enormous thank you to all the editors, staff and board who have labored long hours to sustain this beloved magazine. Thank you to Sarah, Ed, Deborah, Dom and the MPT board for welcoming me so kindly into the fold.

This issue serves as invitation to join me in keeping MPT's feast of languages, cultures, and beauty alive. Like food, art sustains us with much-needed pleasures and comfort daily, as we strive for survival in trying circumstances. You are all humbly invited to take up a seat here any time, to break bread with this magazine – or perhaps, rather, to share tumpeng (the delicious, celebratory, Indonesian rice dish on this cover, by Pratya Aprilana) – together, in the round.

HIRONDINA JOSHUA

Translated by Grant Schutzman from
Mozambican Portuguese

Mozambican poet Hirondina Joshua writes poetry obsessed with the
act of writing itself. It interrogates the written word, not just as tool
of language but as a conduit that contours thought and shapes
perception. Her first collection of poetry, *Os Ângulos da Casa*, is
exponentially self-referential. The poems question themselves, serving
up circuitous questions on the nature of writing, and the boundaries
between self and others. Her writing since then transcends genres,
including her short collection *Como Um Levita à Sombra dos Altares*,
and two more collections of poetry, *A Estranheza Fora da Página*, with
Portuguese writer Ana Mafalda Leite, and *Córtex*.

The poem 'If we're going in let's go in with our whole body and
quickly' distills the thematic tensions present in much of her work,
combining surreal imagery and abstract vocabulary to push the
boundaries of linguistic expression. Seemingly unbridled enthusiasm
is tempered by darkness ('supreme torture'), even as the latter seems
to be overcome by the poem's end. Phonetic similarity between words
('torture' and 'tincture') is employed to examine the relation between
them. Joshua attempts to frame questions that could not otherwise
be said: who are we, what do we want, and how do we get it?

If we're going in let's go in with our whole body and quickly

If we're going in let's go in with our whole body and quickly.
Loyal to the Earth and to this fragment of Humanity. Let's leap
into this earthborn moment without looking back.
Oh supreme torture.
Oh invisible tincture. Indivisible.
If we go in let's drive our whole nail in with the unholy
dimension of our foreignness. Mirrors, we begin from within:
– we divide the darkness and separate the waters.
If we're going in let's go in with our whole body and quickly and
through the front door.

HUMBERTO AK'ABAL

Translated by Michael Bazzett from Spanish; the poet also
wrote these pieces in K'iche' Maya

Humberto Ak'abal (1952–2019) was a K'iche' Maya poet born in
Momostenango, in the western highlands of Guatemala. The
highlands hold mountains covered in cloud forest, fields of maize
and beans, and deep ravines. The connection to place in Ak'abal's
work is palpable; the language seems to arise from the land itself:
stones speak and wooden benches remember being trees. As Ak'abal
himself said, 'My words hold the dampness of rain, / the tears of
morning dew, and it cannot / be otherwise, because they were /
brought down from the mountain'.

There is an elemental immediacy to his poems and a colloquial
straightforwardness in the diction that can allow a reader to arrive
rather quickly at an initial sense of the moment. Yet there is an
ineffable quality to his work that remains elusive, a sensibility that
mixes playful, earthy observations with musings on time and
memory. Given that Ak'abal generally wrote in K'iche' and then
translated himself into Spanish, one is often listening simultaneously
to two versions of a poem, different cadences bridging the colonial
divide. K'iche' Maya has no verb *to be;* past, present and future often
co-exist with a simultaneity that can feel strange to a sensibility
marinaded in linear chronology; dream and memory intermingle.

Ak'abal's work is widely known in Guatemala; his book *Guardián
de la caída de agua* (Guardian of the Waterfall) received the Golden
Quetzal award from the association of Guatemalan Journalists, and
in 2004 he declined to receive the Guatemalan National Prize in
Literature because it was named for Miguel Angel Asturias, whom
Ak'abal accused of encouraging racism, noting that his views 'offend
the indigenous population of Guatemala, of which I am part'.

Landslide

Night tumbles
and darkness falls
into the ravines

where it turns to water
and becomes a river.

Lightning

From time to time
the sky gets scared
of so much dark

and launches lightning
to see if we
are still down here.

To its surprise,
here we are,
trusting
the sky
is still up there.

Opposite: An Indigenous man with grey wispy hair, wearing a
jaguar-skin cap and a red shirt with dark stripes, photographed
from a low angle, looking into the distance

Blue

When I was little
thirst
burned my throat,

until one night I dreamed
my hands opened
a hole in the ground
near an old bridge
and a spring came flowing
clean, flowing
clear.

I cupped my hands and drank;
it quenched my thirst:
not the water,
the color.

INGEBORG BACHMANN

Translated by Alexander Stillmark from German

Ingeborg Bachmann, one of the foremost poets of postwar German literature, wrote in vehement protest against the recent historical past. She studied philosophy at Innsbruck and Graz universities and completed her doctorate on Martin Heidegger's existentialist thought in 1949. Her early lyric poems soon established her reputation as the leading voice of her generation, though she spent most of her adult life abroad. In her poetry the lyrical 'I' has become the 'I' of history: a voice of opposition to the brutal, inhuman era of the Third Reich. The poet's situation in society is one of sorrow and solitude. Pain and suffering fills a world consisting of bleak, stark imagery. This poetry is fundamentally concerned with the uses and abuses of language. Wittgenstein's famous formulation, 'The borders of my language mean the borders of my world,' is tellingly reformulated in her poetological postulate: 'No new world without new language'. The need for a purer, 'cristalline' language without false pathos or contrivance is the sought-for ideal. After her second collection of poetry, *Anrufung des grossen Bären* (1956), she devoted her writing mainly to prose, libretti and essays. Her close relations with Paul Celan, Max Frisch and Hans Werner Henze are well documented in their correspondences, all published after her untimely tragic death in Rome in 1973. Her collected poems have appeared in an English translation in the Zephyr Press (1980).

A Kind of Loss

Jointly used: books and some music.
The keys, the teacups, the bread-basket, linen sheets and a bed.
A dowry of words, gestures, brought with the rest, employed, used up.
House rules observed. Said. Done. And always a handshake.
I fell in love with winter, a Vienna septet and with summer.
With maps, a mountain nook, a beach and a bed.
Performed a cult with dates, declared promises cast-iron.
Adulated a something and was filled with piety for a nothing
(– the folded newspaper, the cold ash, the scribbled note –)
Fearless in religion, for the church was this bed.
Out of the seaview my timeless paintings grew.
From the balcony the nations, my neighbours, could be greeted.
By the hearth, in safety, my hair had its uttermost hue.
The ring at the door was the alarm-bell of my joy.
Not you were my loss,
But the world.

Aria I

Turn where we may in the tempest of roses,
Night is illumined by thorns, and the thunder
Of leaves which so softly stirred in the bushes
Now follows hard on our heels.
Wherever is quenched what the roses ignite
Rain washes us into the stream. O more distant night!
Yet a leaf that struck us drifts on the waves
And follows us up to the mouth of the river.

Go Thought

Go, thought, whilst a clear word wings you
To flight, uplifts and moves you
Where light metals are gently poised,
Where the air is cutting
In a novel sense,
Where weapons speak
Of singular kind.
Champion us there!
The billow carried driftwood up and sinks.
Fever gripped you and lets you fall.
Faith has moved but one mountain.
Let what stands stand; go, thought!
Transfixed by nothing else but our torment.
Be of a piece with us!

JHUMPA LAHIRI

Interviewed for the Non Solo Muse project
Translated by Caroline Maldonado from Italian

The following is an excerpt from the interview 'The Borders of
Identity', part of *Non solo muse* (www.nonsolomuse.com), a project
dedicated to contemporary women poets writing in Italian. The project
is edited by Adele Bardazzi and Roberto Binetti, the interviewers.

NSM: *Nerina's Notebook* is a collection based on the theme of a fictitious
identity or one that is philologically recreated from the authorial voice.
In relation to this I'd like to quote one of the texts where this game of
identity immediately leads us into the question of 'naming':

> 'Anaphora'

> I call whom I love
> by names invented,
> unregistered.
> A secret code
> held tight
> to make that
> relationship mine.

The game recreated from the 'biographical' framework is in some way
a game of mirrors that questions the basis of a traditional lyric subject
and renders it problematical. What value does the theme of identity
have in your work? Does it have an aesthetic value that is fundamental
to the creation of your poetic identity?

Opposite: A woman with brown skin and long dark hair, wearing a black
shirt and a necklace of large pale-blue stones, looks into the camera.

JL: The theme of identity – or rather, the dilemma – is what I have been facing right from the start. On the other hand, now I think about it, I'm not sure that 'identity' is the word I would use, even though no other word comes immediately to mind. Identity shares the etymon of 'identical', and it seems to me that the identical is always a tendentious lie. There is an apparent phonetic identity, for example, in great part also graphic, between the two hemistichs in the first line quoted in the question: 'I call' [chiamo] and 'I love' [chi amo]. However, it seems to me that an accent – or a tone, a detail, a destiny – always comes to rescue my characters, my words (me) from identity, from being identical men, identical women (an identical woman).

In the first books I wrote, still in English, I concentrated on the relationship, always a tense one, between specific identities, one armed against the other: the Indian and the Western, Anglo-American. Out of that came either a double identity, in conflict, or one that dominated, even cancelled out, the other. In fact, I personally felt neither Indian nor American: for each of my aspects it was about expectations imposed from outside, by my family and by the environment I lived in.

When I moved into Italian, my perspective changed together with my identity (I repeat, never identical). In Italian, my first impulse was to significantly muffle, precisely the 'identity' aspect of my characters, maybe to uproot them from the expectations of readers who were themselves rooted in a certain identity, in search of the identical. Above all, I believe I felt the need to definitively escape from the persecution of a perennial question: *where do you come from?*

As much as we can look at it with suspicion, the word *identity* serves as a necessary border: it gives us a boundary to stem the chaos of existential possibilities. On the other hand, I find it an increasingly suffocating concept, a cage, a precarious and dangerous place of landing. Returning to the etymon, the first definition of *identity* is 'perfect equality', and yet for me that word has always alluded to the lack of equality and to imperfection: to the anguish of feeling myself different, alone, excluded.

Nerina, unlike me, is the owner of a plural and hyper-flexible identity. With her I enter an unexplored continent, poetic language, and the question of the specifically literary identity becomes complicated. *Nerina's Notebook* is itself a hybrid text, arising from geometries I had not worked with before. The figure of the triangle is primary. There are three components (the presentation of the book, the poems, the notes) corresponding to three voices (the author, Nerina, Verne Maggio). None corresponds to me. It is a project born out of my long fidelity to Pessoa, from a more recent obsession with Primo Levi's totemic centaur, and from Rimbaud's (marvellously ungrammatical) 'I is an other'.

◆

NSM: In *Nerina's Notebook* the poetic voice expresses itself through a dense system of underlying quotations that consists of a dense system of references to the Italian lyric tradition: from liminary poems, strongly Montalian, to 'an impressive serenism' of some styles chosen, passing via the diaristic prose of Amelia Rosselli. What is your relationship with the Italian lyric tradition? What function does the method of using quotations have in this collection of poetry? What relationship does this collection have with the idea of the canon? Is it possible to identify a relationship between metre (stylistic and linguistic method) and biography in your writing?

JL: Nerina owes nearly everything to the Italian lyric tradition; she arises from my first sustained and crucial encounter with the poetry not only of Montale and Rosselli but with Dante, Pasolini, Bertolucci, Leopardi, Magrelli, Cavalli, and so many others.

As usual, it is reading that triggers the writing. In this case, it released a new form as well – poetry – that I'd never achieved in English. I studied *The Occasions* in depth, mainly to give *Nerina's Notebook* a structure: to make it a book of poetry, in the 20th century meaning of the term, rather than a collection. I hope that the quotes open, amplify, deepen the text. But they also destabilise it. They reveal spaces for a series of cross-references that set up a conversation between Nerina and other poets, between her notebook and other texts, in practice – slightly alchemical – creating two (or more) from one.

This is how another identity of mine enters in this book: the philological. Verne Maggio, the figure that follows and interprets Nerina, her exegete (as Giuseppe Carimandrei was Umberto Saba's exegete) assumes the role not only of editor, but of ferrywoman, of the one supervising and facilitating the transition of those I've talked about. Verne (custodian, protector, scholar) is like the person who accompanies a text from one language to another, who collaborates, opens up the pathways – like translators who are of course philologists and very fine exegetes.

As for the canon, I understand that to be a norm, a binding system, but it is a concept that changes necessarily with time. It, too, is fed by transition, metamorphosis, and it often changes just by virtue of the splits that produce confused debates and successive apparent palingenesis. Nerina is aware of this, but from the outside, perhaps now and again unconsciously. The canon is not a map teaching us how to navigate the world: it is an arbitrary skimming off, proposed and manipulated by the literary ecosystem in every language, every culture, every epoch. It is a mobile, aerial, and geological root that will always be interrogated, and it must transform itself as a people transforms itself, as certain landscapes change very slowly, (though at the same time all of a sudden when one is aware of it) from generation to generation.

NSM: *Nerina's Notebook* is preceded by a preface in which you reconstruct the rediscovery of a manuscript and follow it with the poems that are found there. Following a felicitous tradition of the 8th and 9th centuries, this move creates a narrative framework that prepares the reader for entry into the heart of the text. How do prose and poetry enter into a collusion with one other in this collection and, in a broader perspective, in your novels? Is there a hierarchy between these two 'significant systems'? What kind of value does the hybridisation of several different literary genres assume in this collection?

JL: The poems came first; the frame and the commentary followed. Nabokov's *Pale Fire* showed me the way, even though the frame and commentary dominate that book. As I have said, the interaction that I favour is certainly not one of subjugation, but a transitory dialogue. Anyway, Nabokov alone can't explain this duality. There are all the other authors astride poetry and prose, and among them are so many Italians I admire, from the Dante of *The New Life* onwards: Saba, Pavese, Palazzeschi, Bassani, Landolfi, etc.

My favourite novelist in English, Hardy, moved definitively from narrative to poetry at a certain point. His journey, and that change, has always struck me. My instinct has always been to mix the cards, even though some authoritative readers advised me to lift away the frame and leave only Nerina's voice. In any case, poetry immediately took the upper hand in this project, and the prose portion served as an echo, a shadow.

NSM: *The Notebook* opens and starts from a situation/literary device that moves from micro-story to lyric subject. The one who speaks as 'I' tries to treat their own biography in a variety of texts that one reads as the theme of loss: in the series Disappearances, we read:

> But let's return to the first losses,
> both incidents
> beyond memory,
> two scenes concerning
> my childhood.

What is your view about the existence of an ideal hierarchy between micro-story and macro-history in your poetry? Relating to this, what space is reserved for confessional or diaristic writing? On the other hand, which area provides an opportunity for historical themes with a broader scope? How does the dimension of plurality enter your writing?

JL: Like many books (and like all my Italian writing) Nerina begins in the diaristic space. Paradoxically, only in this book do I succeed in bringing together and welcoming the complete geography of my origins and my life – significantly, under another name, in a form I'd never attempted, in the care of a fictitious scholar, transforming my diary into a rediscovered document. For this reason, *Nerina's Notebook,* from my point of view, breathes more fully than the others. Only the diary, conceived for nobody else, has an analagous aspect that is porous, elastic, and neutral.

Feeling myself to be stateless, I tend to hold macro-history, with which I've always had a nebulous relationship, at bay. Macro-history is a kind of foreign language I must learn, aligned with other terms that are alien to me, like homeland, nation, belonging, and so-called identity. I have already spoken about plurality (of voices, perspectives, forms). I'd add that the other aspect of plurality is singularity, which in turn has to do with solitude, and these are two crucial aspects of Nerina.

NSM: What kind of historical characterisation does the lyric subject adopt? Is it possible to pinpoint even a partial identification between the biographical and historical subject?

JL: Nerina is a palimpsest: she has a shifting personality, ambivalent, ironic-sincere, false-true. If we want to pinpoint one aspect we lose sight of other things.

Life is basically a partial experience. A question of empty spaces, like poetry.

JHUMPA LAHIRI

Translated by the poet from Italian; the poems that follow are
from *Nerina's Notebook*

Cupboard

To make space in the cupboard
overhead, to store our luggage,
I took down the elegant clothes and
assorted hats of the woman who
once lived here, articles washed
and pressed and suited to the past.

They'd been hanging
in the closet when I'd first
seen the apartment.

I grabbed the bony hangers
from the dry cleaners;
the plastic sheathing her
raiments whispered back.

The weight surprised me –
I had to drag them, cupping my hands
beneath the sleeves
as if they contained real armpits.

I called the elevator and unlocked
the door to the basement.
Now in the cold dark they drape
the wobbly daybed

on which I recovered
after they'd opened my uterus:
Then, too, removing something
unwanted.

For Alberto de Lacerda

Dear Alberto,
I think you'd have liked
the smooth sand-coloured
paper wrapped
around your portrait
in black-and-white.

The framer from Trastevere
set aside another job
to greet me, retrieving you
from your grander neighbours –
a row of paintings
you probably despised.

To protect the sheet of glass
measured to fit your photo
he cut a section off the roll
in the middle of the table,
neatly folding flaps, enclosing you.
He asked for fifteen euros.

You became a discreet
package, flat and hard,
unlabelled but destined
to arrive in my study.
You who hated ruckus,
everything superfluous.

Here in blazing silence
you'll see the Roman sky
vast and fickle all the while.
You'll hang by bookshelves
crowded with spines
that stand or rest on their sides.

You don't smile or pretend
to feel at ease. You're as neutral
as your paper wrapping:
immaculate spoils I find
hard to throw away.

PRAKALPA RANJAN BHAGAWATI

Translated by Krishna Dulal Barua from Assamese

Prakalpa Ranjan Bhagawati is an Indian writer and translator who writes in Assamese, the major language of Assam in North-East India. He has experimented with a number of visual poems, eco-poems and sonnets (modelled in the Shakespearean pattern) in Assamese. He has drawn wide critical attention through his first collection of poems titled *Baladharohi Aru Anyanya Kabita* (The Bullock Rider and Other Poems) published in 2021. He is one of the members of a group of poets and critics who streamlined *Parbantarar Padya* (a New Chapter for Verse), by publishing a manifesto in 2020 to consider and reconsider certain issues related to Assamese poetry.

The poem 'Remaining Awake' is one in a series of poems set against the backdrop of terror struck by the Covid-19 pandemic. In a bid to take poetry to the common people, who are generally ignored by most poets, he attempts to catch the rhythm of conversational language in his latest poems.

Remaining awake

Are you awake?
Yes, I'm wide-awake
I'm on my toes sans fever or ache.

What wariness is this wakefulness, after all!
Remaining awake to bid adieu
To one who departs untimely
Without any farewell.
Remaining awake implies remaining alive
To bid adieu to one who departs untimely.

Someone passes by the gateway shouting –
'Beware beware'
I respond with a phlegm-filled throat
'Yes, I'm wide-awake
I'm on my toes to let no one depart
Untimely without being bidden adieu.'

Opposite: An Indian man with a dark chequered shirt, looking
unsmiling into the camera, against a plain background.

UPENDRA SUBBA

Translated by Haris C. Adhikari from Nepali

'Butterfly' is a simple yet arresting poem taken from *Kholako Geet* (2013) – in English, *River's Song* – by Upendra Subba. It insightfully projects a dislocated life in which the speaker is struggling to live, away from his sweet village home, his roots. This projection is, by extension, also a reality lived by most of the urban populace in modern Nepal, also by those who migrated to cities during the civil war, seeking a safer home as well as safer space of learning for their kids.

In the poem, there is a voice of wisdom so compelling, accompanied by a melancholia, and a self-satirising tone that emanates from life's learning, from the disturbing textures of demography in the making, and from unstable contemporaneity. Not fine. Fine. Not so fine. The poem sketches intersections of experiences, followed by grave insights.

I was enticed to translate this poem also by its description of 'chhori' running 'away to catch a butterfly / Fluttering in the yard.' Who isn't fluttering? I asked. I couldn't help but picture 'chhori' as fluttering away, after the butterfly. I also read a hidden sense: That there is a butterfly in all of us that flutters away, enticing us to follow it. This is evident in how the speaker has 'landed' in the harsh realities of urban life. On the other hand, the poet also leaves the reader pondering: Are butterflies really 'not our living'? In short, the poet has employed this ambiguity so economically and in a way that strongly evokes readers' own lifeworld experiences.

Butterfly

My one-and-a-half-year-old daughter
Leaves holding my finger
And runs away to catch a butterfly
Fluttering in the yard –
The butterfly keeps on flying around
And she keeps on following it.

The butterfly flies away from the view
And then she starts crying;
I hold my daughter to my bosom,
Caress her, try to soothe her.
I feel like saying –
'Don't cry, chhori*!
The butterfly is not our living;
It's only a deception like a dream'.

I too have arrived in this city
Leaving my home and village,
My father and mother –
Following and chasing my dream.
And my dream has further eluded me –
It has run away from me.
But like my daughter
I cannot cry
Even though I want to.

*Chhori – daughter

ERVINA HALILI

Translated by Suzana Vuljevic from Albanian

Ervina Halili (b. 1986) is a member of the new generation of young
writers and poets in Prishtina, Kosovo. Halili's beguiling lyricism
ushers the reader into an otherworldly trance with a distinct
philosophical and ecofeminist thrust. As someone who tends to
translate experimental literature by women and other marginalized
writers, I was drawn to the subtle feminist underpinnings of this
collection, which presented a refreshing and welcome departure,
especially in a literary tradition that has long silenced women's voices.
In "The March of the Earth," we encounter planet Earth merging
with the speaker in a cyclical, unceasing process of (re)creation that
takes on patently feminine characteristics. The poem appears in
Halili's fourth book, *Der Schlaf des Oktopus* (Vienna: Edition
Korrespondenzen) – *Octopus' Slumber* – which was published as a
bilingual Albanian-German edition in 2016, and is an expansion of
her third book, *Amulet*, for which she was awarded one of Kosovo's
highest literary accolades. It is a collection of conceptual poetry that
utilizes the figure of the octopus as a symbol and means of exploring
the theme of collective self-destruction, an idea that emerges from
the natural phenomenon of octopuses succumbing to the urge to eat
their own limbs under conditions of extreme stress. Like much of
Halili's other work, the collection is interested in mysticism and
myths inherited and passed down through generations. It is surrealist
in its motifs, concerned as it is with sleep (and sleeplessness),
dream sequences and the associated juxtaposition between (or
inextricability of) reality and fantasy, as well as madness and
the meanderings of the unanchored mind.

Opposite: A young, Kosovar woman with long black hair, resting her
head in her palm, looking contentedly into the camera.

The March of the Earth

Earth, you're nestled in twilight and
from your slumber flows of lava erupted awake in fury
to the drumbeat of a stately march
oozing over the slothful time of budding shoots
and bones saturated in humus-rich soil

follow the rhythm of your vapors and dance with me, Earth
let us lose ourselves
let us lose ourselves
in a delirium

I saved some of your jasmine fragrance, Earth
smear it onto my breasts
and make love to me
till you've pulled my hair straight into your heart

I feed your spawn
I, time of eternity
give birth to the new world

WRAP IT IN BANANA LEAVES

The Food Focus

SAFAK SARIÇIÇEK

Translated by Csilla Toldy from German

In an oftentimes absurd-seeming world, loving can seem like a temporary fortress. But even love did not venture into a black hole. These are some hopefully comical verses describing the first venture of love into the cosmic abyss.

– Şafak Sarıçiçek

Şafak Sarıçiçek is a second-generation immigrant from Turkey to Germany. His parents' language is Zazaki, a dialect of the suppressed Kurdish-Armenian language, and he is bringing a new layer to German from his linguistic heritage. We took part in the Only Question Project, initiated by Ulyanovsk UNESCO City of Literature, conducting a dialogue about our writing. After that I began to translate Safak's work into English. My first translations of his work appeared in *Pamenar Magazine*.

– Csilla Toldy

Humanspaghetti

imagine there would be wormholes
and people disappearing, pulled out lengthwise

like spaghetti

I'd look for you and grab your hand
we'd drift like humanoid spaghetti between space and time.

TEEMU HELLE

Translated by Niina Pollari from Finnish

From poet Teemu Helle: One pitch-black evening I opened my balcony door and noticed something: the silence was so loud. When you stop to listen among all the hustle and bustle, the world shows you its true dualistic nature. Life is the endless dialogue between light and shadow, fortune and sorrow, strength and weakness, body and brain, life and death, and me and you.

Saddle

I opened the door and let in the darkness.
It collapsed on the couch,
lifted its feet on the table and sighed:
'Got anything to eat'.

I took a plastic tray down from the fridge's top shelf
and brought it to the living room, where the darkness
watched, enchanted, a documentary about horses.
I lifted the dome: light in a dessert dish.

The stale earth stank. The darkness
consumed light like a fallen apple
and bemoaned not understanding
how a horse could transport
such a heavy load with its skinny legs.

CATHAL Ó SEARCAIGH

Translated from the Irish by Gabriel Rosenstock

It must be said that Irish-language poetry, as well as the Gaelic poetry of Scotland, have both experienced something of a renaissance in the past half century, yet Celtic languages are among the most threatened of the world's endangered languages. Let us hope that this remarkable blossoming is not what is called in Irish 'biseach an bháis', a last bloom before death.

My grandmother, on my mother's side, uttered those chilling words on her death bed, though she rarely allowed any Irish to pass her lips. Around the time of the so-called Famine, a cataclysmic language shift happened, a Great Silence. (Only one crop failed, the potato: a great variety of foodstuffs was exported under the watchful eye of the landlords' militia and 67 regiments of the British army.) Irish seemed to have no future in a Darwinian world that favoured international buccaneering and the centrality of the market. The oldest literary language in Europe, after Greek and Latin, deserved better.

As wonderfully melodious, enchanting and sustaining as the great Scottish Gaelic poet Sorley MacLean (1911–1996), one can say of Cathal Ó Searcaigh that he is both ancient and new, a mystic concoction of the Bardic and the Beat.

Opposite: A white, Irish man wrapped in a wool blanket, stands in front of a mountain landscape in the daytime, looking to one side.

Apple

Long ago, on my birthday,
my grandfather used to put a notch
in the ridge piece
to celebrate the occasion.
He'd hand me an apple,
a red apple from the tree of knowledge.
It came, he said,
from the loveliest branch in God's own garden.

Today, who can count the notches
engraved in my mind?
I say it with little pleasure
for I've eaten more than my share
of God's rosy apples,
none of which oozed with the juice
of the apples of memory.
I speak from knowledge.

ADRIANA LISBOA

Translated by Alison Entrekin from Brazilian Portuguese

Adriana Lisboa is one of Brazil's foremost novelists and poets. I first came to her work in 2012, when I translated her novel *Crow-Blue*, and have been translating her short stories and poems ever since.

Originally from Rio, a city where nature is omnipresent and land left unattended is quickly reclaimed by the jungle, Lisboa brings a keen awareness of nature to all of her writing, be it in her award-winning novels, short stories or poetry.

The poem 'Bowl' revisits a sub-theme of her work: the poetic investigation of humankind's relationship to the natural world. Lisboa systematically unpicks our anthropocentric vision of the world by bringing other existences into focus and seeking to understand them from within their own experience, all the while acknowledging the impossibility of ever shedding our own subjectivity to inhabit another.

Bowl

as the dog
eats his meal from the bowl
something in the life observing him
wonders what it means
to be here watching him
wonders what it would be like
to exist
and not self-examine all the time
like an obsessive scientist of oneself
what it would be like to run
through the fields without a plough
constantly tilling
every fold of the heart
what it would be like to lick
the bowl
and trust –

Opposite: A Brazilian woman with short hair, hoop earrings, and thick-rimmed black glasses, stood outside with her arms crossed, smiling and looking at the camera.

S. VIJAYALAKSHMI

Translated by Thila Varghese from Tamil

In her two poems, 'Nilam' (land) and 'Marabanu vidhaigalin marana regai' (the death line of genetic seeds), the author Vijayalakshmi addresses the issue of profit-based farming that has been undermining the fertility of the land and man's harmonious relationship with the land, living creatures and nature maintained in traditional farming practices. She points out that the use of genetically modified seeds introduced and enforced by the corporate and government entities have been leading to the loss of plant genetic diversity in recent years. The author contends that 'even when trying to fertilise the land to enrich the soil, they apply poisonous chemicals'.

Many farmers no longer have the option to raise the healthiest and most productive crops by growing the diverse individual varieties from the seeds they themselves had been developing with love and care in their own farms under optimal conditions for hundreds and thousands of years. The widespread use of high-yielding genetically modified seeds with limited nutrient values and the callous exploitation of the land for profit have also been taking their toll on the quality of food production and agricultural biodiversity, which could lead to serious health consequences.

In "Land," the author delineates the deplorable situation in which the farmers shoulder all the labour and responsibilities involved in farming while the authorities decide what to sow in the land so that they can reap the profits. She argues that locally-adapted home-grown diverse seeds are under threat and laments, 'It is on my land that the profit's mega farming occurs'.

In 'The Death Line of Genetic Seeds,' the author presents an alternate picture of how some farmers in remote villages choose to continue their traditional farming practices despite pressures to adopt profit-based farming methods. The farmer, though initially unconcerned, thoughtfully determines towards the end to maintain autonomy in farming by 'turning her inherent faith into a fertiliser' and priming her land 'for the production of plowing tools'. The farmer is presented as a female in this poem to emphasise the primary role and active involvement of women in traditional farming in Tamil Nadu, India.

Land

They are only intent on
seizing my land.
Those who come forward to reap the harvest
are not those who sowed the seeds.
Even when trying to fertilize
the land to enrich the soil,
they apply poisonous chemicals.
What else could those who care about
nothing other than the harvest do?
I am the land.
I water myself.
I have planted seedlings.
I turn my hands into machinery.
What should we name
those who harvest only the benefits?
I can remove the weeds from the field crop.
I can apply the weed killer.
I will choose the fertilizer.
Yet
for selecting which seeds to sow,
the officer's words and commands come into play.
It is on my land
that the profit's mega farming occurs.

The Death Line of Genetic Seeds

She who was scattering grains
on the ground for sparrows and doves
had been unconcerned,
contemplating neither the possibility of
aligning herself with broader circles
nor being rooted in neutrality.
Yet, new rustlings of thoughts
emerging afresh
kept generating sleepless nights
and restless days.
Having transformed into a bat in the daytime
and a vigilant owl at night,
she began transplanting seedlings,
turning her inherent faith
into a fertilizer.
As the hammer of novel experiences
continued to forge into shape
her dearth of wisdom,
her entire acreage
got primed for the production
of plowing tools.

JHIO JAN NAVARRO

Translated by Eric Abalajon from Hiligaynon

In 'Smokestack', Navarro writes about the imposing figures of sugar mills in Negros Occidental, a province in the Philippines known for its vast sugar cane plantations established during the Spanish and American colonial periods. These past decades, this industry has been neglected and deteriorating. To remedy current sugar supply shortages, state officials have resorted to importation, causing drastic increases in the price of the basic commodity. The Ma-ao Sugar Mill mentioned in the poem was shut down in the '90s and as of August 2022, is awaiting auction for scrap metal. Navarro's poem contemplates the postcolonial nation's food security crisis and cash crop economy, which is foremost a question of life or death for peasants and their families.

Opposite: A Filipino man with neat black hair, wearing a white shirt and a red sash, smiles into the camera.

Smokestack

1.

Three sugar mill smokestacks stand sentry in Central Ma-ao.
Like the Father, the Son, and the Holy Ghost, watching over
people from Elga up to La Plata, from Kawilihan down to Guba
reminders of a time past when in the lands of the Araneta clan,
'Money can be picked and shoveled from the ground'.

2.

The smokestacks are giant cigars made of rolled brick
wrapped with iron sheets. But the foundation
that sucks and puffs out has long run out of breath.
Thus, as clouds are widowed by smoke,
the towers are being married by rust.
And in the lands of the Araneta clan it has long been accepted
that, 'For money, even the pick and the shovel must be pawned'.

BIRENDRA CHATTOPADHYAY

Translated by Sayandeb Chowdhury from Bengali

Bengali poetry has been sporadically translated into English, ensuring that some like Rabindranath Tagore and Jibananda Das have been frequently de-anchored from their native language, while some, like Birendra Chattopadhyay, rarely so. This is the first English translation of one of his key poems. The poem is about the abominable misery of hunger and the despondency for 'daily meal' (or the lack of it), uttered as it is, in the voice of the poorest of citizens. Ironically, in this poem the poignancy of desperation assumes the tone of delirious hyperbole bordering on a bizarre sense of humour. Like most modern Bengali writing of that time, this too treats poetry as a site of encounter between a participatory planetary present and a more personal belonging in the complex realities of the Global South. In this case there is an unambiguous socialist cry against the perpetuity of hunger and an explicit revolt against the prevalence of romanticism in poetry. This poem is from the collection *Ulukhor*, and was published in 1954.

Give me bread[1]

It may turn out to be bogus, burnt or smelly
But it still tames the hunger in my belly.
Our sermon is 'Give me bread'; 'Bread', we say!
In return, friend, take whatever you may.
Samarkhand, Bukhara are but ration paltry
I can expend the liberty of my country.

For two meals of burnt bread a day
I can wake up before the sun makes hay,
I can catch the stormy sea by its mop,
Or uproot the Karakoram from its top.
Hurt, grief, conscience are but matters faded,
For bread, I can squander the eyes of my beloved.

1   The Bengali word roti used in the original commonly means the handmade
flat cake made from fresh wheat dough, which is a staple across the
Subcontinent. But I have used *bread* to give it the wider connotation of being
a *basic meal*; and also because bread – the baked breakfast item of most of
Europe, which travelled with it to South Asia and is widely available – is
also called roti in several languages, including Bengali.

ZAFIR SETU

Translated by Mohammad Shafiqul Islam from Bengali

Zafir Setu (b. 1971) is well-known as a poet of soil and soul, light and love, and sound and sight. His poetry leads readers to intensely mull over myth, history, philosophy, tradition, and civilisation. Deeply rooted in his own land and culture, Setu is on a par with the distinguished transnational poetic voices, who demonstrate world consciousness in their poetry. The two poems titled 'My Family by the Haor' and 'This Condensed Colostrum' are from the poet's latest collection, *Ami Karachgaach* (I Am a Karach Tree). The collection, engaging with myth and metaphor, paints the portraits of the people of the haor, the low-lying land in the north-eastern region of Bangladesh. The karach tree, which is a special kind of tree growing in the haor, has a great and long-lasting bond with the haor people.

Almost everywhere in Bangladesh, villages are disappearing with the aggression of urbanisation. As a result, clothes, food, and culture are going through transformation, and people are distancing from tradition and roots, losing self-identity too. The poem 'My Family by the Haor' shows how a farmer feels while eating steaming rice mixed with ghee. It touches readers for its candid rendering of the simplicity of haor people. Similarly, 'This Condensed Colostrum' exhibits myth, folk, and tradition through symbols and metaphors. Village people believe that the condensed colostrum of cows is very useful for both people and calves – it is propitious to pour some colostrum onto water for the wellbeing of river and fish. Consequently, the cows give more milk and give birth to lots of calves as fish breed innumerable eggs. In the poem, the poet invites his beloved to go back to childhood so that they can take colostrum together in order to keep hale and hearty. The mood, image, and implications of the two poems invoke deep thoughts about life and nature, and the poet's love for life and nature is eternal.

My Family by the Haor

As you pour ghee on the plateful of steaming rice,
an astounding love billows.

Steam rises from rice, and I deeply feel you.
When you stretch on the yard to clasp a cow,

I feel I love both equally.

This Condensed Colostrum

Again let's drink this yellow condensed colostrum,
smelling raw and fresh.

Let's have the smell of this milk like kheer.
If you want, let's swim and float.

Together with the fish, let's drink, you and I,
this yellow condensed colostrum.

Opposite: A Bengali man with short black hair, wearing glasses and a
black collared shirt, standing outside in the daytime.

AW PRIATMOJO

Translated by Ian Rowland from Indonesian

'A Menu for Mother' responds to the idea of resilience in family ties as expressed through food; both the intimate nature of home cooking, and also the role of specific foods in bonding both families and the wider community, through symbolic meaning for certain foods.

The author was inspired by his own mother, herself an expert cook. Living away from the parental home, in the city, he continues to miss her cooking.

The poem seeks to conveys this constant sense of contact – how the mother's presence manifests itself in foods encountered during the author's life in the city – social gatherings celebrating life events, and even the snacks eaten in the office.

Two of the foods in the poem have particular resonance in traditional Javanese life, and represent unbreakable links between the protagonist and their mother.

Wajik is made of glutinous rice, coconut milk and sugar. Found at every Javanese wedding, its stickiness echoes the hope for a close bond between the couple. Preparing it is time- and labour-consuming, calling for patience and cooperation. It symbolises a long-lasting marriage founded on the collaboration of the spouses.

Jenang is a toffee-like confection made from glutinous rice flour, coconut milk and sugar. Jenang putih is white, sweetened with cane sugar, representing the male. The addition of red-brown palm sugar, representing the female, during cooking produces jenang abang, symbolic of the union of mother and father through the child.

Considered together, they symbolise new life, and are present at any ceremony celebrating a birth.

Opposite: An Indonesian man with short black hair, wearing a white collared shirt, sits against a white background and smiles into the camera.

A Menu for Mother

1. The White Jenang and the Red

In that pot Mother cooked up her prayers.
The rising smoke accompanying her wishes.

Father was the white jenang.
And with a splash of palm sugar
the red jenang was Mother.

The dining table was where all dreams were sown.
And all memories stored.

2. Gudeg

Memories floated in the coconut cream
among jackfruit green. Seeping into
the hard-boiled eggs, until I swept off to the city.

They were in the fast-food chicken and
the coffee shop drinks too.

Her prayers had followed me to town.
swaying among the vehicle fumes.

Jostling for space in
the rush hour trains.

3. Lemper

The scent of shredded chicken rose
from the ledgers
whose figures stuck like sticky rice.

I flipped the numbers
in the books

to show:
the furthest distance between me and her.

I wanted to wrap it in banana leaves
pinning both ends
with palm rib slivers.

Carry them to work each day, for lunch.

4. Wajik

I built this home from sticky rice
with pandanus-scented walls
and sticky stains of remembrance on the table.

I say to my wife who stirs the pan at the hearth:

'Even in that flaring flame I see her'.

LEE JENNY

Translated by Archana Madhavan from Korean

The partaking of food is often an act of care and comfort, of both emotional and bodily nourishment. In South Korean poet Lee Jenny's work, food is often juxtaposed in unusual and startling combinations with the abstract, bringing about a vital concreteness to the complexity of emotion we feel by virtue of being human.

'On Mornings I Drink Corn Soup' is one of Lee's earliest poems, written 17 years ago, following the sudden passing of the poet's loved ones. Through rhythm and repetition – mainstays of Lee's poetics – the poem becomes an incantation, an ardent prayer to conjure the faces of those we've lost. With the chant of 'kernels kernels kernels', the poem beats like a heart and throbs like a wound, transforming these simple fruits into kernels of grief and longing that float through a bright, warm world.

Opposite: A close-up selfie of a Korean woman with long dark hair, looking unsmiling into the camera, with the sun shining brightly white behind her on a sandy beach.

On Mornings I Drink Corn Soup

On mornings I drink corn soup I
need a table
so it may as well be a round and warm table and I
need a chair
so it may as well be a round and warm chair and I
need a bowl
so it may as well be a round and warm bowl and I
need a person
so it may as well be a round and warm person and
the corn kernels are yellow
kernels kernels kernels bob-bob-bobbing in the soup and
with every kernel I think of faces dead disappeared erased and
now they're gone the kernels I eat
round and warm kernels I eat
there's soup too the soup's good too
the corn kernels are yellow
kernels kernels kernels please don't spill
kernels kernels kernels spill and I'll be sad
like a kernel I care about what I say
even now in the morning I write in my notepad a list of all the kernels
I ought to care for
how can I already know these kernels I've never once seen?
kernels kernels you can see the kernels
because you believe you can see the kernels
kernels kernels kernels corn kernels are yellow
round and warm kernels kernels kernels
I want to believe maybe I'll see them some time
I do miss them a bit the kernels kernels kernels

N.A. MANSOUR

Faqoos

My first memory of faqoos is sunshine and a cardboard box.

My parents are reaching into the box they've just barely bought from a roadside vendor, and are pulling out the short, thin, pale green vegetable, and holding it up to the light so I can see the thin fuzz growing on ridges down its length. They shake the faqoos to loosen the red-brown dirt clinging to this almost-invisible beard, and wipe them against the hems of their shirts before handing one to me.

'Like a cucumber', they tell me, and I heed their instruction, eating it like I would a fresh cucumber. As I crunch down from one end to the other, I silently relish how faqoos is not like a cucumber at all.

On that day, it didn't make sense for me to ask for anything else to eat with faqoos, like a handful of olives or bread. We'd been driving through Arriha, on the Palestinian side of the Jordan River Valley. We'd stopped to buy bananas on the side of a road and to smell tobacco plants in a field, at the invitation of their caretaker. We even pulled over so my parents could walk my four-year-old self through a cotton field and show me what it took to make my clothes. It was a trip where, once we'd reached our destination and shook off the layer of dust adhering to our own bodies, we'd shuffle from house full of relatives to house full of relatives. My parents were pacing me (and themselves), maybe delaying the inevitable dance of guest and host for their own sake. They'd rather be here, on the road, in a field, and I was their excuse.

Because faqoos is a little sweet and often more curvy than a cucumber, I've never felt the urge to substitute it for a cucumber in salads or sandwiches. But the question itself is never broached, because, when I am in Palestine or Jordan, rarely does faqoos make it home to my kitchen. It is caught, suspended in space between my home and its home: the vine. I'm afraid that the longer it's been since it's been picked, the less of that crispness will survive to make it to my gnashing teeth.

The vegetable market's already a buffer period as it is and the faqoos season is short, only lasting a few short weeks in June (and neatly coinciding with apricot season).

Today, faqoos makes me paranoid; I don't mention it much outside of my family. I used to ask after it, wherever I went, largely in vain – I've never seen fresh faqoos outside of Palestine or Jordan. As with all Palestinian foodways, there's also the fear that speaking about it means our colonisers will hear us speak passionately about a food or a custom, produce a facsimile, and place it squarely in their historical narrative, denying we ever had a role in its cultivation. Colonisers aside, I've become wary of what happens when we consciously peddle our cuisines, packaging them in bright flowery fonts and changing the words we use to describe something. It does something to the soul, to be constantly translating for an audience that only seeks to consume and commercially capitalise on our food. It strips my memories to the bone: keep the sunlight, discard the thrice-re-used cardboard box the farmer uses to package three kilos of faqoos. Maybe go further: Get rid of most of the three kilos and throw in some hype. *This is your new favorite ingredient. Forget cucumbers.*

But I don't want to forget cucumbers. A good, short cucumber is one of the great joys in life. Beautifully crunchy and either sliced or whole, they are an essential item in every Palestinian child's school lunch. The cucumber exists alongside faqoos, unaware of market competition. But in the act of translation, the way many of our ingredients are "discovered," there is only space for one.

I don't tell anyone about cucumbers either. I resist the urge to write the flashy piece for the cooking section of a newspaper or magazine that tells you you've been eating cucumbers wrong, and here is something from my culture to be gifted to yours, to be gifted to people I don't know, people I can't hand a cucumber to myself. I translate myself, make myself more human, and I am giving you a gift, to be greedily snatched up by some readers. I am not given much in return.

When I am tempted to write the easy pitch to a food magazine on faqoos for some quick cash and notoriety, I remind myself that I don't even know how to translate the term into English. Some editors' insistence on an English term is to make it intelligible, to make readers want to try the food, but it's also to assert that faqoos or any other food has already been vetted. It's why in cookbooks, particularly of food from the Arabic-speaking world, even if the name of a dish is in Arabic-rendered-to-English-script, there's a name in English, a description of the dish in a few words. To translate, not the name of the dish, but the dish's entire being, from its material form into a collection of words is to make it palatable. It's showing it has been vetted. For faqoos, I might be asked to look for a scientific name, to demonstrate faqoos has been slotted into the knowledge system of western science.

To translate the word faqoos is not the same as translating a larger tract; a poem, for instance, where you can choose to perhaps leave some of the text untranslated, where you can hold on to the names. To translate a name is to choose to re-name it and risk changing its very essence. I have to rewire some synapses, form associations with the new name; the effort falls mostly on me. The bare minimum I can do when writing about food is to refuse enforcing a language hegemony onto single words that do not need translation. But to take a step beyond with my writing practice is to refuse to translate or transmit it, unless I find places for faqoos to exist that are safe, that mirror the confines of my own heart.

YASHODHARA RAY CHAUDHURI

Translated by Mamata Nanda from Bengali

Yashodhara Ray Chaudhuri is a prolific and highly respected Indian author based in Kolkata, India. Her poetry represents her widespread experience as a high ranking civil servant, a celebrated public intellectual and an avid traveler. She writes on the themes of love, alienation, relationships and ongoing social and political issues, often expressed through everyday objects and deceptively simple scenes of daily existence. Her poetry revolves around Indian social and cultural traditions and uses references to classic literature, customs and colloquial vocabulary. I was drawn to her poetry for this particular reason: the deep emotions expressed through daily existence. The poem presented here has been taken from her book *Abar Prothom Theke Poro*, meaning 'read it again from the beginning'. Written when she was pregnant (around 1999), it reflects the intense emotions she was going through in her day-to-day life at the time. The collection deals with the theme of creation in life – especially childbirth – as well as childhood and society.

Yashodhara has written several poems that reflect on our relationship with food and cooking, the relationship between poverty and written words and the close connection between food and emotional well-being. In 'The Days of Milk and Yogurt', I see a woman, stuck in a mundane life, feeling left out, experiencing ambivalence and seeking comfort from simple things in life. The descriptions of the objects in the fridge felt very solid to me and I wanted the opportunity to convey this realism to an English-reading public in a way that maintains the vividness of the imagery, without losing its poetic rhythm or the slightly sinister, ambiguous atmosphere of the scene.

The Days of Milk and Yogurt

The air of suspicion is close, my darling!
I open the fridge to a gentle scent of vanilla,
A fat and wobbly packet of milk,

A pot of yogurt,
Standing behind a loaf of bread in half darkness
Is the solitary cold pot of yogurt

Acidity comes close,
My fury against you comes close,
So I have to keep going to the fridge with a glass in hand.

Milk, the antacid, cold milk
The majestic fridge lovingly pours
For me, like a mother...

The scent of vanilla drips from its breasts.

PEDRO DE JESÚS

Translated by Dick Cluster from Spanish

Over the past twenty-five years, Pedro de Jesús has published short
stories, a novel, criticism, and poetry in Cuba and abroad. He lives
not in Havana but in a town of some 30,000 people in the interior
province of Sancti Spiritus. His stories, which began to appear in the
1990s, were among the first published in Cuba to deal explicitly with
queer sexual identities. He has twice won his country's major literary
award, the Premio Alejo Carpentier, once for fiction and once for
criticism, as well as the award of La Gaceta de Cuba for short
fiction and the Raúl Ferrer prize for poetry; as a philologist, he is
a corresponding member of the Academia Cubana de la Lengua.
Throughout his career as primarily a prose writer, de Jesús has been
quietly writing poetry in diverse forms, ranging in form from sonnets
to free verse to something like epigrams, and in theme from love and
sex to language to politics and philosophy. This poem comes from
his 2016 collection *Granos de mudez*, Ediciones Luminaria, Sancti
Spiritus. On the theme of food and cooking, readers might be
interested in his story, 'Partying at the Maitre's House', in the
collection *Vital Signs* (tr. D. Cluster, Diálogos Books, 2014).

Opposite: A Cuban man wearing a light shirt and a ring on each hand,
sitting in a wooden armchair with his legs crossed, next to a white
ashtray.

Untitled

While setting the table, the lover
seems to weave, unweave the cloth,
and, antediluvian alchemist,
cast the glass and metal.
When he pours water
and serves fruit and grains,
primeval rock splits open
offering up its sweetness,
earth udder fills and spouts
spurting
so the childhood of Man
in the lap of the World
can begin.

When the beloved—who does not love—sits down
to eat,
it seems that glass and metal are not enough
to bring the universe to his mouth.
The grains grow scarce.
The water, surely, is no eternal gift.
The beloved gobbles up the lover wholesale
without pausing over subtleties of seasoning,
and the lover, uneasy, discovers
that no tablecloth, no music, no candelabra,
can hide the primordial need
for that meal.

When the beloved—who does not love—sits down
to eat,
everything seems suddenly final,
as if the end of Man
and the World
has begun.

KUSHAJIM

Translated from the Classical Arabic by Salma Harland

When Will You Come to Eat?

When will you come to eat?
   The table has been set
And the chef has adorned it
   How rain dresses gardens in marvels.
It is spread before us,
   Heaped with delectable dishes:
A roasted kid
   With 'usban,
Garnished with minted legumes
   And tarragon;
A plump-breasted pullet
   That we selectively bred;
Grouse and chicken
   Braised in a tagine;
Fried samosas
   Overlapping with tardin;
Red-dyed eggs
   Served with olives;
Palm pollen like strings of pearls
   Nestled in a jewellery box;
Open-faced sandwiches
   Brushed with an oily relish
That whet and tempt
   Every indulgent appetite
With bites like pearl shavings
   Kneaded with ambergris;

A sharp cheese
For a filling spread;
An ornate knife
For cutting and slicing;
Vinegar that flares up noses
Even before it is unsealed;
Aubergine burani
That will enchant you;
Asparagus unlike any other –
And I know you have relished many;
Musk-scented lawzinaj
Doused with sugar;
Cooked wine that comes
In dastija jugs and bottles;
A dimple-chinned cupbearer
With voluptuous promise,
Fiery eyes,
And honeyed words;
And a singer who coos like a turtle dove
sweet tunes never heard before.
So, why would a jilted lover
Far from his love's abode
Rather drink himself out of his senses
Than come join us?

On Kushajim's 'When Will You Come to Eat?', or How to Hold a Banquet Fit for an Abbasid Caliph

By Salma Harland

Kushajim (c. 902–970) was a celebrated tenth-century Arab Shiite poet, master chef, and polymath of Indo-Persian origin. He served in the court of Sayf al-Dawla, the founder and ruler of the Emirate of Aleppo from 945 to 967, and arguably the most famous ruler in Islamic history. Though a poet of considerable range, Kushajim is best known as a pioneer of ekphrastic epigrams (maqṭuʿāt al-waṣf): short yet highly-complex monothematic poems characterised by hyper-realistic sensory depictions of carnal and earthly topics. In these poems, Kushajim vividly chronicles social, intellectual, and culinary aspects of court life under the Hamdanid dynasty, detailing the harem with its cross-dressing male and female dancers, concubines, and odalisques; the various musical instruments used in the Abbasid era to entertain caliphs and their guests; numerous native and foreign foodstuffs and recipes; the social etiquettes of sharing food and wine; the traits of coveted courtiers and boon-companions; the art of gift-giving; the wide variety of plants and geometric designs found in courtly gardens; and indoor pastimes and outdoor sports. Kushajim's known works include *Etiquette of the Boon-Companion* (Adab an-nadīm), *The Characteristics of Music* (Khaṣāʾiṣ aṭ-ṭarab), *Book of Snares and Game* (Kitāb al-maṣāyid wa-l-maṭārid), an influential collection of poems, and a collection of epistles.

Kushajim often incorporated macaronic and hybrid words in his poetry, mixing Persian in his Classical Arabic verse. In 'When Will You Come to Eat?', he uses old Persian words such as tardin, burani, and dastija, to list a few (see the following paragraph). Although premodern and contemporary literatures do not comment on the reason why he did so, his motivation might be ascribed to biographical and sociolinguistic factors. Though born in Palestine, Kushajim was of Indo-Persian origin. His great grandfather al-Sindi Shahik was the chief security minister of Caliph Harun al-Rashid (c. 766–809). Born out of wedlock, al-Sindi (literally 'the Indian') was named after his Indian-born mother rather than a father – the latter of which was more traditional. It is also important to note that the Abbasid Caliphate flourished as a multicultural melting pot with eastern reaches that stretched to include Sind (modern-day west India) and Fars (modern-day Iran). Thus, inserting Persian vocabulary into Classical Arabic poetry was not uncommon, dating back to the eighth-century Arab poet Abu Nawas.[2] Still, knowledge of the Persian, Indian, and Byzantine ways (especially cultural and culinary practices) was indicative of status in the Abbasid era. A court poet and courtier, Kushajim often flaunted his multilingual and multicultural knowledge, particularly evident in his poems on food, clothes, perfumes, and the harem.

In 'When Will You Come to Eat?', Kushajim throws a lavish banquet for a friend suffering from a broken heart, to mitigate his sorrows. Along with handsome cupbearers and exquisite singers, the banquet – furnished by the master chef of Sayf al-Dawla's court himself – has many delectable dishes from the farthest stretches of the caliphate to please all palates. Using *The Book of Cookery* (Kitāb al-ṭabīkh) by Kushajim's contemporary author and food critic Ibn Sayyār al-Warrāq, and *The Doha Historical Dictionary of Arabic*, I have compiled here a description of each dish. May it bring this ekphrastic feast of the senses to life.

2 Lara Harb, 'Persian in Arabic Poetry: Identity Politics and Abbasid Macaronics', *The Journal of the American Oriental Society*, vol. 139, no. 1, Jan.-Mar. 2019, pp. 1+.

Kushajim's Banquet

Aubergine burani (Persian) – aubergine slices fried in a mix of olive and sesame oils, dressed with Nabataean murrī (fermented sauce), spices, and rue leaves.

'Usban – roasted liver wrapped in herby caul fat and crispy salted intestines.

Samosas – savoury pastries filled with a mixture of minced lamb, Nabataean murrī, onion, leek, and aromatic spices and fried in olive oil.

Red-dyed boiled eggs

Open-faced sandwiches – slices of oven-baked bread brushed with olive oil relish.

Cheese – mouthwatering fiery ḥirrīf cheese.

Asparagus – boiled and drizzled with olive oil and Nabataean murrī, served hot.

Olives – black and green olives in sweet olive oil with added salt and thyme.

Date palm pollen – fresh date palm pollen of the male date palm, an aphrodisiac.

Vinegar – aged grape vinegar.

Main Dishes

Roasted kid – slow-roasted juicy kid seasoned with olive oil, salt, and pepper; served with a dipping sauce of mustard seeds and sweetened raisins.

Pullet – slices of pullet breast grilled to succulence, drizzled with sweet almond and cucumber sauce, and garnished with fresh chopped thyme, mint, and basil.

Chicken and grouse tagine – thin slices of grouse and chicken meat baked in sweet and sour pomegranate juice and olive oil drizzled with Nabataean murrī and vinegar mustard then garnished with asafetida leaves, thyme, sumac, and juniper berries.

Tardin (Persian) – baked triangular meat patties made with lean meat, onions, and spices, drizzled with olive oil and served with mustard.

Desserts

Lawzinaj (Persian) – sweet pastries stuffed with a mixture of almonds, pistachios, rose water, cloves, and white cane sugar, drizzled with almond oil and a dusting of sugar then perfumed with musk.

Drinks (Served in Persian dastija, a large glass jug with two handles)

Cooked wine (halal) – an aged and sweet-smelling wine made from grapes, honey, spring water, and saffron, boiled on an open fire until the alcohol content is evaporated.

Kushajim's 'When Will You Come to Eat?' had a striking effect on Baghdadi caliph al-Mustakfī bi'llāh (908–949), as Arab historian and polymath 'Alī ibn al-Ḥussain ibn 'Alī al-Masʿūdī (c.896–957) vividly details in *Meadows of Gold and Mines of Gems* (Murūj al-dhahab wa maʿādin al-jawhar). One day, the anecdote goes, al-Mustakfī held a lavish banquet where men of letters vied to present their best verse and prose on food and drink. Al-Mustakfī immediately fell in love with two of Kushajim's poems recited by one of the attendees. 'When Will You Come to Eat?' was one of them, the other a poem on asparagus.[3] After hearing the former, al-Mustakfī eagerly said: 'We want this exact banquet, as per this exact description. Bring it to us, for we shall eat none today but what you have just described'.[4] Regarding the latter, he gave his orders: 'We do not have any [foodstuffs] of this description in this country, and we shall request that Muhammad ibn Tughj al-'Ikhshīd brings us some of this delight from Damascus'.[5] This is but one of many historical records that show the far-reaching influence of Kushajim's gastronomic poems on court life and culinary choices in the Abbasid era and beyond.

---

3 My translation of Kushajim's poem on asparagus, 'We Have Spears with Crooked Ends', was run bilingually along with three others in 'Four Gastronomic Poems', *Ancient Exchanges (Diversions)*, Autumn 2021.
4 'Abū al-Ḥasan al-Masʿūdī, *Meadows of Gold and Mines of Gems* (Murūj al-dhahab wa maʿādin al-jawhar), IV, edited by Kamāl Hassan Marʿī, al-Maktaba al-ʿAsriyyah, 2005, p. 288, my translation.
5 Al-Masʿūdī, ibid, p. 292, my translation.

LENA YAU

Translated by Colaboratorio Ávila from Spanish

Food is an obsession for Lena Yau, one of Venezuela's foremost contemporary writers. From her poetry to her novels, Yau sees food at the center of relationships, identity, and memory. Yau served as literary advisor for *El sabor de la eñe,* a glossary of literature and gastronomy produced by Instituto Cervantes in 2011. She has published three poetry collections – *Trae tu espalda para hacer mi mesa* (Gravitaciones, 2015; Sudaquia, 2021), *Lo que contó la mujer canalla* (Kalathos, 2016), and *Bonnie Parker o la posibilidad de un árbol* (Utopía portátil, 2018) – the novel *Hormigas en la lengua* (Sudaquia, 2015; Baile del sol, 2021) and the short story collection *Bienmesabes* (El Taller Blanco, 2021; Sudaquia, 2022).

'Twenty years is nothing' is taken from *Trae tu esplada para hacer mi mesa* [*Bring Your Back to Make My Table*], in which the taste, look, feel, sound and smell of food mingle with lust, deception, heartbreak, loss and reencounters.

Born in Caracas, Yau now lives in Madrid. She is one of the six million Venezuelans who have left their country during the two decades under the 'Bolivarian Revolution'. The original title of the poem, 'Veinte años no es nada', is a famous line from Carlos Gardel's 1935 tango 'Volver' [To Return], which presents a traveller who longs to return to his home and love yet fears the reencounter with his past. Both Gardel's traveller and the Odysseus reimagined in Yau's poem capture the mixed emotions towards a lost home of the Venezuelan diaspora.

Twenty Years Is Nothing

He returned home.
His wife welcomed him.
On a splintered melamine plate,
the fossil of a veal escalope,
his favorite meal.
Ulysses' eyes filled with tears.
He reached into his pocket for a lotus leaf stolen on that island.
He devoured it.
Two seconds later his memory had emptied.
Of those banquets with Calypso and Circe not even the scent
remained.
He lovingly kissed Penelope and sat down to dine,
taking pleasure.
His tongue had forgotten other homelands.

Opposite: A Venezuelan woman resting her chin on her hands, wearing
a thin metal watch, looking into the camera.

MICHELLE C. BUSS

Translated by Lúcia Collischonn from Brazilian Portuguese

'Mother Joana's House' is a poem published in 2018 in Brazil, as part of the book *não nos ensinaram a amar ser mulher* (we were not taught how to love being women). It's the third book of poetry by the author, with poems written through personal or observed experiences on being a woman, and the diversity that this encompasses. As the title highlights, considering the challenges that women live through in our societies, the book delves into the great challenges one faces to love and accept fully the woman in each one of us. This collection of poems intends to reflect upon plural aspects and perspectives on what it means to be a woman, putting aside fixed ideas and considering it an ever-changing concept, bringing both feminism and the variety of possibilities for femininity. The title of this poem, 'Mother Joana's House', is an expression in Portuguese that refers to a house where everyone is welcome, but also where everyone does as they please without much respect for others. The English translation of the book – by Lúcia Collischonn – remains unpublished.

Mother Joana's House (everything goes)

There go the mouth napkins,
the stored apricots,
caramelized nuts...

There go the talks about amenities,
the eggplant *bruschette*,
the pesto sauce,
the unfunny jokes, the daily laments...

There go the three bottles of *vinho verde*,
more conversations about sex, about the weather,
about the stock market...

There go the toilet paper rolls,
the frailties and the mediocrity,
all the dirty floor cloths...

They go
There they all go...

And she stays.

She always stays behind...
With a pile of dirty dishes, a broom to sweep
and a very strong dose of generosity
with undertones of neediness.

ANNA YIN

Translated by the poet from Chinese

In 2021, when I served as judge for a poetry contest, I was very impressed by a poem talking about 'hot pot'. I was born in Hunan province in China. At home, especially in winter, we enjoy hot pot a lot. We are famous for eating all kinds of food accompanied by red peppers. Folks regard girls from Hunan as 'Sister Red Pepper' because of the food we are used to, and also our hot blood that makes us seem brave and bold.

At a poetry workshop this year, when we were asked to write a self-portrait poem, I immediately thought of red pepper and love relationships.

Lately, when I want to teach students about shape poetry, I use this poem to illustrate how a text can be revised as a shape poem, and it works well. Of course, the poem I wrote in Chinese was not shaped thusly. I have written other food poems in both Chinese and English; i.e., I have a special feeling about apples and pears because of my Chinese culture. However, these special meanings are hard to translate into English. I have also written two other shape poems in English, but in Chinese, I have never written one. Other strategies would be needed. Living in a multicultural country like Canada, I might give it a try someday.

Self Portrait as Red Pepper

In
your
hot pot,
you add me
first, then pour
fresh spring water
to boil. You say in
this way the flavor
comes out slowly.
Do I? after all these
years, my red is red,
is red...yet my skin
becomes shriveled
and dry. Soaking in
the heat-emanating
water — I swell and
spread long-overdue
flare and flame, and
wonder who would
spurt out scarlet
thrilling love
songs as my
rosy spicy
memory
blends
into
this
hot
p
o
t.

The night is long,
the pot eventually
cools down.
In the dark, I
know it is time
        to move on.

FEDERICO GARCÍA LORCA

In 1927, Spanish poet Federico García Lorca published 'August'
(Agosto) as part of an early collection of poems titled *Canciones
(1921–1924)* [Songs, 1921–1924]. In this poem, he explored nostalgia
through Spanish summer images, comparing Andalusian sunsets to
summer fruits and its pits. The poet is particularly remarkable in his
ability to portray children who flash grins as hard as ear of corns at
each other while eating brown bread and rich moon, the latter chiefly
introducing surrealism in his verse.

In 1919, García Lorca had moved to Madrid's Residencia de
Estudiantes, where he met Nobel-prize winner Juan Ramón Jiménez,
an Andalusian poet like him, and made friends with surrealist
painter Salvador Dalí and filmmaker Luis Buñuel. Many scholars
have analysed the influence they had on the poet; however, I see this
as a two-way street. In 'August', for instance, I read García Lorca's
powerful line 'An afternoon with the sun inside' ('El sol dentro de la
tarde') as an inspiration for Jiménez's 'Light with the time inside'
(La luz con el tiempo dentro), published three decades later.

August

August.

Peach and sugar
Against the sunset,
An afternoon with the sun inside
like the stone in any fruit.

The ear of corn keeps
its yellow, hard grin intact.

August.

Boys eating
brown bread and rich moon.

FU HAO

Translated by the poet from Chinese

This poem was written on the 11th of April, 2020, since it has been
a tradition in China for men of letters to write a poem on their own
birthdays to celebrate. It was an unusual birthday for the author, as
it was during the Covid-19 pandemic period, and all Chinese people
were suffering the same fate. The poem is translated into English by
the author himself and has never been published before. In order to
aid readers of different cultural backgrounds in better understanding,
the author-translator would like to add a couple of notes here
concerning some allusions in the poem:

1. According to Confucius, the Chinese sage, one grows to know one's
   destiny by the age of fifty.
2. In Cantonese, the pronunciation of the word for lettuce is
   'sang-coi', of which a homophone means 'to make a fortune'.

Opposite: A Chinese man with thin-rimmed glasses, wearing a dark
blue shirt, sitting in an armchair next to a bookshelf and looking into
the near distance.

Birthday

It has been seven years since I knew my destiny.
Providence cannot be disobeyed.
Without my knowing that old age is coming,
old age will come anyway.
The pandemic is still in full swing,
so I dare not go out to eat,
nor dare I order take-out
because I'm afraid of getting infected without symptoms.
I have to go to the balcony
and gather a head of lettuce I have grown with my own hands
to congratulate myself
and hope that, as the superstitious Cantonese say,
after eating it I may make a fortune.

CRISTINA MORANO

Translated by Layla Benitez-James from Spanish

Originally from Madrid, Cristina Morano is deeply rooted in the poetry community and landscape of Murcia and has lived there for over thirty years. 'A Year Without Rain' comes from her collection *Climate Change* (Bartleby Editores, 2014) and is tightly woven from that landscape and mixed with elements from La Crisis, Spain's economic crisis lasting from 2008–2014.

For translating this poem in particular, it helped to live in Murcia for two years and get a sense of how the environment shaped Moran's palette of poetic images. On a literal level, the rain here is often filled with dust from the Sahara which covers windows and blurs edges in her poem, rather than being cleansing. Talking with Morano was also important in understanding how the human suffering which *Climate Change* points us to is not our mere human condition; it's not some neutral and inevitable state of being which all humans must pass through, like death. Rather, these poems are spun out of the suffering of economics and those who are left to bear the brunt of inequality on our natural world.

While the ethos of these poems could find common ground among veins of ecopoetics, these are not completely natural disasters, they are manmade and their causes are known; here it is a misdistribution of wealth which allows individuals to be tossed by the forces of the market. *Climate Change* opens with an epigraph from Yannis Ristos' poem, 'Greekness', in which the landscape 'clenches its jaws. There is no water. Only light'. That image is interpreted with a quiet surrealism in "A Year Without Rain."

A Year Without Rain

Dusty city . . .
Ramón Gaya

There's always been sun, but light?
The light has gone to dust;
it doesn't sing about the day
but dampens window shine
and the corners' brilliance,
bending around itself, heavy, clumsy.

All the animals grazing
in the streets have been drowning
in this grey light. We too
look skywards, taking stock:
– Can you see anything? – Not even an insect.

Winter without rain:
what will we do without your fruits.

Opposite: A selfie of a Spanish woman with long dark hair in a white
t-shirt, wearing lipstick and glasses, looking without smiling into
the camera.

SHEN HAOBO

Translated by Liang Yujing from Chinese

Shen Haobo, born in Jiangsu in 1976 but currently based in Beijing, is the author of eight poetry collections in Chinese, and the CEO of Xiron Books, the largest private publisher in China. As a publishing tycoon, he has produced numerous bestsellers, more than any other publishing companies in China. However, as a poet, his reputation remains controversial – not only because he used to be known as the leading figure of the Lower Body Poets, an avant-garde poetry group in the early 2000s noted for its erotic writing, but because he was a major polemicist during the 1999 Panfeng Polemic, a large-scale poetic debate on the Chinese poetry scene between two camps – the 'intellectual' and the 'populist/unofficial' poets. That debate was extremely messy. To put it simply, Shen sided with the 'populist/ unofficial' camp, which reveals his own poetics: a preference for colloquialism, earthly aesthetics and the unofficial stance (all in the Chinese context). Therefore, 'Lower Body' and 'unofficial' became the two labels that made Shen a countercultural figure in his early career. His first collection was banned in 2004 and he ran abroad for a few months to avoid possible arrest. After this short exile, Shen returned to Beijing and gradually grew into a very successful publisher. His later poetry also became complex in style and varied in subject matter, but always with a rebellious temperament. An excerpt from Shen's poetic sequence 'Wenlou Village Accounts', translated by Liang Yujing, is available in *MPT*, No. 2, 2017.

Opposite: A Chinese man with short black hair, wearing glasses and a black jumper, standing outside against a white wall.

At a Chateau in Bordeaux

The owner was introducing us
to his home-brewed Merlot.
He, a Christian, said
red wine was the blood of Jesus.
Then I heard, outside the window,
the vines all over the hills,
lifting their wizened arms,
chant together, 'No, our blood!'

Dwelling in Detachment

You Can Be the Last Leaf, Maya Abu al-Hayyat (translated by
Fady Joudah), Milkweed Editions, 2022
Review by Mayada Ibrahim

Maya Abu al-Hayyat's *You Can Be the Last Leaf*, translated by poet-
translator Fady Joudah, is a collection of prose poems in the shape
of thoughts, notes or letters, deceptively using vivid, cinematic
images of quotidian life to destabilise one's very sense of location.
They form layers and reverberate, but they tend to fracture, creating
a sense of losing one's ground, of being suspended between places.

The collection spans twenty years and is her US debut. Abu
al-Hayyat is known for her multifaceted practice. She is a novelist,
a poet, a children's stories writer, a literary translator, an actor in a
popular drama about modern life in Jerusalem, and a director of the
Palestine Writing Workshop, which teaches storytelling and creative
writing to children and teachers.

'I lived in ten homes,' she says in an interview on Cultural
Resource (Al-Mawred Al-Thaqafy). 'I consider this the basis for my
personality, my language, and my transitions between different
genres'. She was born in Beirut to a Lebanese mother and a Nablusi
father who was a member of the Palestine Liberation Organization.
She lived in Jordan, then Tunisia, and when she moved to Palestine,
she first lived in Nablus, then Ramallah, where she now works, and
finally Jerusalem, where she now lives. *You Can Be the Last Leaf*
opens with:

> None of the many houses I lived in
> concern me.

The poems appear in reverse chronological order. One can trace a poetics of detachment that manifests at first as the sense of observing from a distance – 'I'm the saline earth that walks on the curb | surveys the city's crowds' – but there are lingering links to dreams and people. There's a repeated reference to a 'you' which seems to address a person: 'Tonight | these things don't wound me | your player heart, the young women around you'. There is a 'you and me' who might have been 'building a city'. During her twenties, Abu al-Hayyat tragically lost her lover to the Israeli occupation. He was shot dead on the first day of the second intifada. The poem 'Mahmoud' addresses a 'you' who was martyred and with whom the speaker might have had a child named Mahmoud.

In earlier poems, there is a sense of ownership – 'This is my country, that is my sea | and here is my elegant lie' – that is tenuous and gradually disappears midway through the collection. The detachment becomes more explicit:

I live in other people's stories
like a rock suspended in space:
it doesn't drop and can't.

The 'you' becomes larger and more opaque, sometimes god- or state-like. 'You rented houses for us in paradise', 'We thanked you when we were sick', 'Politely we thanked you as our teacher | had instructed'. Perhaps the diffusion of the 'you' over time has to do with the way it becomes harder to pin one's discontents on a given person or thing; with the illusory nature of self. Perhaps it also creates more room poetically. Nowhere is that clearer than in 'Whistling', the poem I found most arresting, which disorients any sense of self. There is a departure from the interpersonal, and a move towards possibilities that glimmer in further and unlikely directions.

Do you see this hole in my neck?
Not sure if it was a bullet or a word that did it.
But I'm certain two lips passed over it
and left a whistling behind.
And also a rustle
whenever I turn
to the future or the past.

The poems are their most powerful once this language of
detachment sets in, once it morphs into something more complete.
Fady reflects such detachment by diluting the subject and bending
the syntax. In 'My House', the Arabic line 'the house that belongs
to me' becomes simply 'my house' and is nestled into the sentence:
'I will raise my house on the backs of horses'. In 'Almost Dead,
Almost Alive', he sidesteps centering the 'I':

Naked I carry my casket on my shoulder,
wear it to soirees and special events,
take it or when I write a poem
about love, war, and heartless images.

Abu al-Hayyat often describes her experience of living in
Jerusalem in terms of being and not being. 'I live in Jerusalem but
it is not a lived experience'. For one thing, there is a constant fear
that the residency permit will not be renewed at the end of each
year. 'That's why the idea of a home is problematic. Because home is
not permanent'. Abu al-Hayyat therefore probes the underpinnings
of anything that claims to be complete or encompassing. There is
a resistance to restricting the poems to a single time or place.
One would hope that her work doesn't find itself classified under
reductive labels, as any literature from Palestine often is. As Joudah

puts it in his essay, 'My Palestinian Poem that *The New Yorker* Wouldn't Publish', 'To reach English, Palestine passes through a corrupting prism, and is often received as ethnography'. Abu al-Hayyat embraces tenuousness and seeks stability within:

> Each time an opportunity arises for me to not believe in one thing or another I smile from ear to ear
> to let all this freedom in.

Repetition as Transformation for Change

Habitus, Radna Fabias (translated by David Colmer),
Deep Vellum, 2021
Review by Esther Heller

'Habitus' in sociology is defined as habits, skills, and bodily
dispositions that promote distinct orientations in the world. It
can be thought of as a speaker that can sound out the relationship
between society and embodiment with a starting voice that can
either be that of the individual or collective or of both all at once.
This multichannel speaker quality is akin to debut collection *Habitus*,
by award-winning poet Radna Fabias. The book has been translated
from Dutch to English by David Colmer, who recently won the
James Brockway Prize.

Fabias was born on the Caribbean Island of Curaçao and moved
to the Netherlands at seventeen. This movement from Curaçao to
the Netherlands, and all the spaces in between, is cinematically cut
into three pieces: 'view with a coconut', 'rib', and 'demonstratable
effort made'.

Each section consists of a cacophony of voices that speak in
multiple volumes and languages. This is recognisable from the
beginning poem, 'what I hid', which hints at different languages
that are used to navigate the island:

the native language
the official language
the unofficial language
the unofficially segregated supermarkets
the unofficially segregated schools.

The repetition of 'unofficial' here is understood as referring to the use of a language that is not spoken, but lived and embodied by individuals in Curaçao society.

Colmer in his translator's notes points out that 'Curaçao is a polyglot society with Dutch as the administrative language, a large majority of the population having Papiamentu as their mother tongue, and widespread use of English and Spanish'. Fabias's relationship in this environment of languages is that her usage of Spanish is not just from the geographical proximity to Venezuela and the Dominican Republic, but also from the Castilian Spanish of the Dutch education system. Whereas with English her ear tuned and picked up 'American English from TV, music, the tourism industry, the British English taught at school, the Patois of Jamaican immigrants, and the lilting voices of her relatives from St Martin', according to Colmer.

Colmer shares that for Fabias it was crucial that the English in the book be familiar to readers in Curaçao, and not sound British, nor Australian (where Colmer is from). Navigating this space of multiple languages is something that the translated collection achieves successfully in various ways. In some cases, it is brought on not solely through translation but through Fabias's own choices, such as in the opening epigraph of the third section with the Biggie Smalls line from his song 'Juicy': 'it's all good, baby baby'.

Another instance of this is in the poem '(great-)grandmotherly advice', which through the repetition of the word 'never' and the phrase 'better off' highlights a specific usage of language, and stressing of urgency, which is connected to the advice of a Caribbean great-grandmother. The closing lines of the poem:

never trust a man don't
trust anyone trust me

further articulates a social context that also recalls the church ('Put no more trust in man, who has only the breath in his nostrils. Of what account is he?' – Isaiah 2:22). Curaçao has a large Roman Catholic following. In fact, the hum of the church vibrates through the collection in both imagery and sound.

A consistent leitmotif in *Habitus* is the concept of advice which is heard, given, solicited (e.g. by a fortune teller), and received. This advice also comes in the form of the travel guide poems, that translate a deeply entangled and problematic relationship between the island and tourists.

The first, titled 'travel guide I', opens with a conditional statement:

you can dive there if you are not afraid of depth

If you type 'Curaçao' into a search engine, the first things that pop up are images of idealistic sandy beaches and palm trees. On YouTube, there are countless videos with titles like 'Curaçao the Ultimate Travel Guide', 'What to Experience in Curaçao', 'Top Five Things to do in Curaçao', etc.; these videos are to a large extent made by white content creators and couples visiting the island.

Most of these videos do not talk about the historical context of the island, which is present and visible in the guides by Fabias. As she writes in 'Travel Guide III':

you can visit the churches, which are actually the same as the churches you already know |
but brightly coloured
to distract from
the shame and the blood
on the walls

The poem addresses this lack of reckoning with the present and past colonial history of the island by tourists and visitors. The short and precise choice of line breaks adds an emphasis that does not mince words, even though it is in the language of a tourist guide. Fabias's arrangement of this language strips it of its phantasmagoric delusion and adds a depth that is revelatory and meaningful.

Fabias's attentive direction of the poems gives *Habitus* a sequential montaging arrangement, that is not linear but reflects a movement of different points in time, breaks, rhythm, enjambement, and sound. There is a clear visual language in the blank black printed pages that separates the sections of the collection. These read like black frames that punctuate to a close one section, yet also open another section. An example is the first section's final poem, 'closing scene', which is located at the airport. It describes the motions of going through airport security before departure:

the final inspection shows that i'm not wearing anything explosive
under my skirt i am not dangerous
the hollow doesn't get inspected

The poem communicates an unaddressed void, yet in the silence, there are decibels heard in this space that reflect assumptions, and hence profile you as dangerous. Flash-forward to the closing poem of the last section, 'demonstratable efforts made'. It ends on a long list similar to end credits, describing all the things that come with the emptiness of having to appear not dangerous in return for a welcome from:

the well-fed cows
the xenophobia
the freeways
the efficiency

Habitus addresses racism, colonialism, gender, love, loneliness, being Black in the Netherlands and much more, through a potent repetition. This repetition is ceaseless in the way the poetry moves, draws, raptures, and transforms understanding in incredible, mind-opening ways.

NOTES ON CONTRIBUTORS

ADELE BARDAZZI is the co-founder of «Non solo muse» (www. nonsolomuse.com), «Italian Poetry Today» (www.italianpoetrytoday.com) and the «Gender & Authority» Network (https://www.torch.ox.ac.uk/gender-and-authority).

ADRIANA LISBOA is the author of widely translated fiction and poetry books. She won the José Saramago Prize for *Symphony in White* and an honorable mention in the Casa de las Américas Award for *Pequena música*. Her novel *Crow Blue* was chosen as a book of the year by *The Independent*.

ALEXANDER STILLMARK is Emeritus Reader in German at University College London. An elected member of the Austrian P.E.N. Club, he has twice been awarded a translation prize by the Federal Chancellor's Bureau, Vienna. His translations of Georg Trakl and Ivan Turgenev have appeared in *MPT* New Series, Nos. 8, 11 and 16.

ANNA YIN, Mississauga's Inaugural Poet Laureate, has authored five poetry collections and a book of translations: "Mirrors and Windows". Her work has appeared in *The New York Times, Queen's Quarterly, China Daily, CBC Radio*.

ALISON ENTREKIN has translated many of Brazil's most beloved and iconic literary works, earning her a number of honours, including the 2019 NSW Premier's Translation Prize. She is currently working on a new translation of *Grande Sertão: Veredas* by João Guimarães Rosa, with support from Itaú Cultural and the Australia Council.

ARCHANA MADHAVAN is a translator of Korean literature into English. She is currently working on translating Lee Jenny's debut poetry collection, *Maybe Africa* (Changbi, 2010). She resides in San Jose, California.

AW PRIATMOJO is an Indonesian author whose poetry and short stories have been published on various platforms. He is one of the founders of Nyalanesia, a platform for promoting literacy in Indonesia.

BIRENDRA CHATTOPADHYAY (1920–1985) was a prominent, powerful and impenitent Bengali poet of socialist causes and small presses, of petite poems and direct proclamations, of unsung miseries and postcolonial doubts.

CATHAL Ó SEARCAIGH (b. 1956) is the last native speaker of the Min 'a Leá dialect of Donegal Irish. He is one of the great Irish-language poets of the modern era. The poem *Úll* (Apple) is from his latest book *An Tír Rúin* (Arlen House 2022).

COLABORATORIO ÁVILA is a transatlantic translation collective formed by Katie Brown, Claudia Cavallín, María Gracia Pardo and Raquel Rivas Rojas to translate into Venezuelan Spanish and share Venezuelan women's voices in English.

CRISTINA MORANO is the author of *La insolencia* and *Hazañas de los malos tiempos*, among others. 'Poet', appeared in English translation (Waxwing, 2017), and her debut novel, *Las Novias*, was published April 2022.

CSILLA TOLDY is the writer of three poetry books and a short story collection. She translates contemporary fiction and poetry from Hungarian and German.

DICK CLUSTER's recent books include *The History of Havana* (OR Books), and translations of Gabriela Alemán's *Family Album* (City Lights Books) and Paula Abramo's *Fiat Lux* (FlowerSong Press).

ERIC ABALAJON is a lecturer at UP Visayas, Iloilo. Recently his poems were included in *Sobbing in Seafood City* (Sampaguita Press, 2022) and *Footprints: An Anthology of New Ecopoetry* (Broken Sleep Books, 2022).

ERVINA HALILI is a poet from Prishtina, Kosovo. She is the founder of the Rilindja Archive (1945–1999), an online repository of multimedia materials that document the work of the Yugoslav-era Albanian-language daily newspaper and publisher, an initiative for which she received the 2021 Democracy Award. Her most recent book, *Eyes Not Mine (Nuk janë sytë e mi)*, was released earlier this year.

ESTHER KONDO HELLER is a Kenyan German poet, creative/theoretical critic, and filmmaker. They are a Barbican Young Poet 18/19, Obsidian Foundation fellow, and Ledbury Critic 21/22 and are currently doing an MFA in Poetry at Cornell University.

FEDERICO GARCÍA LORCA (Granada, 1898–1936), poet, playwright, and one of the most internationally celebrated Spanish authors, was murdered in the early days of the Spanish Civil War.

FU HAO works as research professor at the Institute of Foreign Literature, Chinese Academy of Social Sciences in Beijing and writes poetry and academic papers bilingually in Chinese and English.

GABRIEL ROSENSTOCK (b.1949) is a bilingual poet, haikuist, tankaist, translator, novelist, playwright, essayist, short story writer, children's author and in the words of Hugh MacDiarmid a 'champion of forlorn causes'. Dozens of his books are available online.

GRANT SCHUTZMAN is a poet and translator. He is particularly fascinated by multilingual writing and that which has been deemed the untranslateable. His poetry is forthcoming in *Eunoia Review*.

HARIS C. ADHIKARI, Assistant Professor of English and Professional Communication at Kathmandu University, is a widely published poet and translator from Nepal. He has authored three books of poetry and literary translation.

HIRONDINA JOSHUA is the author of several collections of poetry, including *Os Ângulos da Casa* (2016) and *Córtex* (2021). She has appeared in literary festivals in Portugal and Spain.

HUMBERTO AK'ABAL (1952–2019) was a K'iche' Maya poet from Guatemala. His book *Guardián de la caída de agua* (Guardian of the Waterfall) was named book of the year by Association of Guatemalan Journalists and received their Golden Quetzal award in 1993. In 2004, he declined to receive the Guatemala National Prize in Literature because it is named for Miguel Ángel Asturias, whom Ak'abal accused of encouraging racism. Ak'abal, a recipient of a Guggenheim fellowship, passed away on January 28th, 2019.

IAN ROWLAND translates Indonesian literature into English. His publications include a short story by Hadi Winata in *Portside Review*, poetry by Erni Aladjai in *Chogwa Zine* and a short story by Pratiwi Juliani in *BODY Journal*.

INGEBORG BACHMANN (1926–1973), was born in Klagenfurt, Austria. She studied philosophy at the universities of Innsbruck and Graz. In 1952 the Gruppe 47 awarded her their annual literary prize. Her first collection of verse *Die gestundete Zeit* appeared in 1953.

JHIO JAN NAVARRO was born and raised amid the sugarcane fields of Brgy. Don Jorge L. Araneta, Bago City, Negros Occidental. He writes poetry in English, Filipino and his mother-tongue, Hiligaynon.

JHUMPA LAHIRI is a bilingual writer and translator. Her most recent publication in English, *Translating Myself and Others*, was published in Spring 2022 by Princeton University Press. Her most recent publication in Italian, *Racconti Romani*, was published in Fall 2022 by Guanda.

KRISHNA DULAL BARUA is an Indian writer and translator. He has translated poems, short stories, novels and essays of a few major Assamese writers into English. He won the Katha Award for Translation in 2005. He has also rendered a number of Bhagawati's Assamese poems into English.

KUSHAJIM (*c.*902–970) was a celebrated Arab Shiite poet, master chef, and polymath. His works vividly chronicled Abbasid court life at the heart of the Islamic Golden Age.

LAYLA BENITEZ-JAMES is a National Book Critics Circle fellow and NEA fellow in translation, as well as the author of *God Suspected My Heart Was a Geode, but He Had to Make Sure*.

LEE JENNY is an acclaimed South Korean poet. She made her literary debut in 2008 and has since published four poetry collections. Most recently, Lee was awarded the 2021 Hyundae Munhak Prize. She resides in Geoje Island.

LENA YAU (Caracas, 1968) specialises in the combination of food and literature. She has published a novel, a short story collection and three poetry collections. Her work has appeared in multiple anthologies. She lives in Madrid.

LIANG YUJING is a lecturer at Hunan University of Technology and Business, China, who has published eight books of translation, including *Zero Distance: New Poetry from China* (Tinfish Press, 2017).

LÚCIA COLISCHONN is a Brazilian-German translator and PhD candidate in Translation Studies at the University of Warwick. She specialises in Exophony in creative writing and translation, multilingualism and L2 translation.

MAMATA NANDA is a retired academic based in London. She has always loved reading poetry and translating between Bengali and English. She is the author of the first official Bengali translation of Maya Angelou's collected poems (Parampara Books, Kolkata, 2020) and her completed collection of Sylvia Plath's poems is coming out in Spring 2023.

MAYADA IBRAHIM is a New-York based translator, editor and writer, working in Arabic and English. Her translations have appeared in *Circumference Magazine* (US), *Banipal* (UK), and *Willows House* (South Sudan).

MICHAEL BAZZETT is a poet & translator. He is the author of four collections of poetry, and his verse translation of the Mayan creation epic, *The Popol Vuh* (Milkweed, 2018), was long-listed for the National Translation Award and named one of the best books of poetry in 2018 by the *New York Times*. A folio of his Ak'abal translations recently received the Gabo Prize in Translation, from *Lunch Ticket*.

MICHELLE C. BUSS is a writer and researcher from the countryside, South of Brazil. She currently lives in front of the sea in the Northeast along with her intempestive sweet cat, Miwá.

MOHAMMAD SHAFIQUL ISLAM is author of two poetry collections, most recently *Inner State*, and the translator of three books. His work has appeared in numerous international journals and anthologies. Dr Islam is Professor of English literature at Shahjalal University of Science and Technology, Sylhet, Bangladesh.

N.A. MANSOUR is a historian of books, art and religion who writes about food and culture.

NIINA POLLARI is the author of the poetry collections *Path of Totality* and *Dead Horse*. She is also the translator of Tytti Heikkinen's *The Warmth of the Taxidermied Animal*.

PEDRO DE JESÚS (b. 1970) is a prize-winning author of poetry, fiction, and criticism. He lives in the town of Fomento in central Cuba.

PRAKALPA RANJAN BHAGAWATI is an Indian writer and translator who writes in Assamese. He has drawn wide critical attention through his first collection of poems titled *BALADHAROHI ARU ANYANYA KABITA (THE BULLOCK RIDER AND OTHER POEMS)* published in 2021. He is a member of a group of poets and critics who streamlined *Parbantarar Padya* (a New Chapter for Verse), by publishing a manifesto in 2020 to consider and reconsider certain issues related to Assamese poetry.

PRATYA APRILANA is an illustrator based in Bandung, Indonesia. She is a former architect who found her way into illustration later in life. She currently works freelance and enjoys illustrating for children's books.

ROBERT BINETTI holds a DPhil in Medieval and Modern Languages from the University of Oxford. He is co-founder of «Non solo muse» (www.nonsolomuse.com) and «Italian Poetry Today» (www.italianpoetrytoday.com).

S. VIJAYALAKSHMI, a teacher by profession, is actively engaged in the Tamil literary field, penning poetry and articles on literary and social issues. She has contributed poems and essays to several Tamil magazines, and has to her credit four published books of poetry, one book of short stories, and two collections of essays. An ardent feminist, Vijayalakshmi continues to participate in literary and social forums that explore the place of women in society.

ŞAFAK SARIÇIÇEK is a law clerk in the Karlsruhe district. He's published five poetry books, and won various literary awards and scholarships, most recently the Klagenfurter Literaturkurs of the Bachmann Prize.

SALMA HARLAND is an Egyptian-born, England-based literary translator who works between Arabic and English. Her works have appeared in *NCW's Emerging Translators Anthology* (2022), *ArabLit Quarterly, Ancient Exchanges*, and elsewhere.

SUZANA VULJEVIC is a historian, writer and translator who works from Albanian and Bosnian, Croatian, Montenegrin and Serbian. She holds a Ph.D. in History and Comparative Literature from Columbia University. Her work has been published in *Asymptote, Eurozine, Exchanges*, and elsewhere.

SAYANDEB CHOWDHURY teaches literature and cinema, writes on culture and politics, and has authored *Uttam Kumar: A Life in Cinema* (Bloomsbury, 2021). He is most readily found at https://sayandeb.in/.

SHEN HAOBO (b.1976) is a Beijing-based Chinese poet, who used to be the leading figure of the Lower Body Poets, an influential but controversial poetry group in the early 2000s.

TEEMU HELLE (b. 1982) is a Finnish poet and the author of 6 collections of poetry. The seventh collection will be published in the fall of 2022.

THILA VARGHESE lives in Canada, where she works part-time during the academic year as a Senior Writing Advisor at Western University. Her translations of Tamil literary works have been published in *World Literature Today, Modern Poetry in Translation, Indian Literature, Metamorphoses, National Translation Month, Columbia Journal,* and *Asymptote*.

UPENDRA SUBBA, a popular Nepali poet and writer, is one of the crusaders of Creative Anarchy literary movement in Nepali literature. Recipient of numerous awards, he has authored three books of poetry and a collection of short stories.

YASHODHARA RAY CHAUDURI is a Bengali author and French to Bengali translator residing in Kolkata. She has published over 40 books, and has also edited anthologies. She has received many prestigious literary awards in India.

YOLANDA MORATÓ (1976) is a translator, poet, and senior lecturer of English at the University of Seville, whose last publication is *Libres y libreras. Mujeres del libro en Londres* (2022, 2nd edition).

ZAFIR SETU, Professor of Bengali Literature at Shahjalal University of Science and Technology, Sylhet, Bangladesh, is a poet, essayist, and fiction writer. He has authored more than thirty books of poetry, short stories, novels, and essays.